Spring Flowers, Autumn Moon

THE POEMS OF LI YU (LI HOUZHU)

春花秋月何時了:
李煜（李後主）詞英譯
/ 林健一，楊大維

Bilingual Edition

TRANSLATED BY JIANN I. LIN AND DAVID YOUNG

EDITED BY RICHARD K. KENT

PINYON PUBLISHING

Montrose, Colorado

Cover Art: Photo 259282903 | Chinese Painting © Elinacious | Dreamstime.com

First Edition: January 2024

Pinyon Publishing
23847 V66 Trail, Montrose, CO 81403
www.pinyon-publishing.com

Library of Congress Control Number: 2023949987
ISBN: 978-1-936671-94-6

Spring Flowers, Autumn Moon

CONTENTS

INTRODUCTION

Li Yu's life story (937-978) is an extravagant one. He belonged to the ruling family of the Southern Tang kingdom, succeeded to the throne and ruled briefly, then became a prisoner of the more powerful and warlike Northern Song dynasty, and was eventually executed by poison.

This vivid arc, from prince to prisoner, from rule to ruin, is reflected in his poetry. Ineffectual as a ruler, he loved and celebrated court life, with its parties, dancing, drinking and trysts. Later, having lost his kingdom, he came to know sorrow, homesickness, and the need to reconcile his melancholy with the passage of seasons and the fragility of life.

The forty-four poems presented here, arranged chronologically, reflect his dramatic story, which is also well-known in China through operas, plays, and even children's books. His poems, always in the *ci* (song lyric) form, which required setting words to the melodies of popular songs, are admirable for their skill, economy, and grace. They manifest an extraordinary artistry and originality. Taken together they offer an unusual autobiography in glimpses, the record of a highly dramatic life at the cusp of dynastic change.

This represents the fourth such collaboration by Jiann Lin and David Young. Our earlier collections include Yu Xuanji, Du Mu, and Su Dongpo. We liked to feel that we were collaborating with the original author too, over many centuries. While Li Yu is the least well-known of this group to English readers, he is a great favorite of the Chinese. Readers wishing to explore his world and work further may want to seek out and consult Daniel Bryant's *Lyric Poets of the Southern T'ang* and Susan Wan Dolling's *A River in Springtime: My Story of Li Yu in Myth and Poetry*. Sadly, Jiann Lin died shortly after completing work on this manuscript, and I would like to dedicate the book to his memory.

David Young
Oberlin, Ohio
November, 2023

1. 浣溪沙

紅日已高三丈透，
金爐次第添香獸，
紅錦地衣隨步皺。

佳人舞點金釵溜，
酒惡時拈花蕊嗅，
別殿遙聞簫鼓奏。

1. To the tune
Sands of the Silk-Washing Stream

Bright red morning sunlight rises,
    piercing the palace curtains.

All night charcoal in animal shapes
    replenished the incense burners.

The red brocade carpet is wrinkled
    from hours of dancing maids.

The lead dancer, still at it,
    was losing her golden hairpins,

tipsy and limping,
    picking up flowers to smell, over and over,

while drums and flutes could still be heard
    from another royal court.

2. 玉樓春

晚妝初了明肌雪，
春殿嬪娥魚貫列。
笙簫吹斷水雲間，
重按霓裳歌遍徹。

臨春誰更飄香屑？
醉拍闌干情味切。
歸時休放燭花紅，
待踏馬蹄清夜月。

2. To the tune
Spring in the Jade Pavilion

Their evening makeup just applied,
    the palace maids look bright, snow-white.

Inside the gorgeous palace
    they line up, single file.

The little orchestra of pipes and flutes
    carries as far as clouds and waters.

They play the wonderful "Rainbows and Feathers" dance
    all the way to the end.

At the Early Spring Pavilion
    servants spread fragrant powder, carried by the breeze.

High on the music and the wine,
    caught up in feelings, I tap the railings.

Time to go home, the banquet's over,
    make sure to snuff the candles.

Sound of my horse, clopping in the moonlight
    through the stillness of the night.

3. 更漏子
(一題溫庭筠作)

金雀釵，
紅粉面，
花裏暫時相見。
知我意，
感君憐，
此情須問天。

香作穗，
蠟成淚，
還似兩人心意。
珊枕膩，
錦衾寒，
覺來更漏殘。

3. To the tune
Night Song of the Water Clock

Your golden sparrow hairpins in my hair,
    your face powdered red, even and smooth.

We hide among blossoming shrubs
    just for the chance of brief meetings.

You know my deep affection,
    I'm grateful for your tender love.

Heaven will witness
    my firm commitment.

Incense smoke rising like wheat,
    candles forming tear drops.

Our love holds true
    between us.

Coral pillow, velvet and satin,
    cool brocade, silken quilt.

Awake in the dead of night,
    counting the hours till daybreak.

4. 菩薩蠻

花明月暗籠輕霧，
今宵好向郎邊去！
剗襪步香階，
手提金縷鞋。

畫堂南畔見，
一向偎人顫。
奴為出來難，
教君恣意憐。

4. To the tune
Bodhisattva-like Barbarian

Bright flowers, dim moonlight,
    traces of light fog.
A perfect time tonight
    to meet up with her lover.

Climbing the stairs in her stocking feet
    among the fragrant flowers.
Tiptoeing, carrying
    her gold-embroidered shoes.

They're meeting on the south side
    of the sumptuous palace.
She hugs and cuddles in his arms
    shivering.

"It's hard, my lord, this sneaking out
    to meet with you.
Still, do as you please—
    don't hold back!"

5. 菩薩蠻 (2)

蓬萊院閉天台女，
畫堂晝寢人無語。
拋枕翠雲光，
繡衣聞異香。

潛來珠鎖動，
驚覺銀屏夢。
臉慢笑盈盈，
相看無限情。

5. Another to the tune
Bodhisattva-like Barbarian (2)

Amid the fabulous courtyards,
    a woman lovely as a goddess
takes an afternoon nap in the hall of paintings—
    no sound of anyone.

Her raven hair on the pillow
    shines like floating clouds;
her embroidered robe gives off
    a magical perfume.

I come to her stealthily
    jangling the string of pearls at the door,
waking her up from a dream
    of silver folding screens.

Her tender face breaks gradually
    into a joyful smile:
we gaze in each other's eyes
    with a love that has no limits.

6. 菩薩蠻 (3)

銅簧韻脆鏘寒竹，
新聲慢奏移纖玉。
眼色暗相鉤，
秋波橫欲流。

雨雲深繡戶，
未便諧衷素。
宴罷又成空，
魂迷春夢中。

6. Another to the tune
Bodhisattva-like Barbarian (3)

Bronze reeds make clear and melodious music,
    along with the chatter of cold bamboo.
New tunes performed by slender fingers,
    shifting gracefully.

Her eyes send secret glances
    as we seduce each other.
Bewitching passions
    flow like autumn ripples.

Love arrives like clouds and rain
    behind the elegant palace doors;
it came about so suddenly
    we had no chance to harmonize.

The banquet's over,
    everything feels empty.
And the soul wanders lost
    in the midst of bright spring dreams.

7. 喜遷鶯

曉月墜，
宿雲微，
無語枕邊歌。
夢回芳草思依依，
天遠雁聲稀。

啼鶯散，
餘花亂，
寂寞畫堂深院。
片紅休掃儘從伊，
留待舞人歸。

7. To the tune
Joyful Oriole Flies Away

Dawn, and a bright moon setting,
persistent clouds thinning out.
Speechless against my pillow,
disturbed by longing,
I wake from a dream of fast-growing grass,
missing my love so deeply.
The geese sound sparse, flying away.

The orioles sing and scatter,
the flowers wither and fall.
The hall of paintings is silent,
likewise the depths of the courtyard.
Don't sweep up the fallen blossoms.
Let them lie there until
my dancer comes home again.

8. 長相思

雲一緺，
玉一梭，
淡淡衫兒薄薄羅，
輕顰雙黛螺。

秋風多，
雨相和，
簾外芭蕉三兩棵，
夜長人奈何！

8. To the tune
Eternal Longing

Hairdo piled like a cloud,
jade hairpin like a weaver's shuttle.
A very simple dress, a very thin skirt,
a pair of eyebrows, knitted in concern.

Autumn winds, blowing hard,
mixing with heavy rain.
Outside the window, banana trees—
the night is long, nothing I can do.

9. 一斛珠

晚妝初過，
沈檀輕注些兒箇。
向人微露丁香顆，
一曲清歌，
暫引櫻桃破。

羅袖裛殘殷色可，
杯深旋被香醪浣。
繡床斜憑嬌無那，
爛嚼紅茸，
笑向檀郎唾。

9. To the tune
A Casket of Pearls

She's finishing her evening makeup
dabbing on sandalwood lipstick.
She turns and shows her tongue between her teeth
then sings a little song
that parts her cherry-blossom lips.

Her thin silk sleeves, perfumed, are stained bright red.
Cups of precious wine have filled her body.
Sprawled on the bed's embroidery,
so coddled and impossible to resist,
she chews to shreds a reddish wildflower,
aims at her lover, smiles and spits.

10. 子夜歌

尋春須是先春早，
看花莫待花枝老。
縹色玉柔擎，
醅浮盞面清。

何妨頻笑粲，
禁苑春歸晚。
同醉與閑評，
詩隨羯鼓成。

10. To the tune
Midnight Songs

When searching for spring, start early.
Enjoy full blossoms—don't wait till they wither and fall.
Let wine-cups be lifted by jade-white hands
and full cups of raw wine be brimming.

Why not laugh loudly and often?
In the royal garden spring lasts a little longer.
Let's get drunk together, gossiping,
composing poems to the beat of a double-headed drum.

11. 後庭花破子
(或為馮延巳作)

玉樹後庭前，
瑤草妝鏡前。
去年花不老，
今年月又圓。
莫教偏，
和月和花，
天教長少年。

11. To the tune
Flowers of the Inner Court

Jade trees rise in front of the inner court;
fragrant herbs are at the makeup mirror.

Last year's flowers still haven't faded;
this year's moon is round and bright.

Don't let favoritism rule you;
make sure you harmonize the flowers and the moon.

Then heaven will let you enjoy your youth
for a long, long time.

12. 漁父

浪花有意千重雪，
桃李無言一隊春。
一壺酒，
一竿綸，
世上如儂有幾人？

12. To the tune
Fisherman's Song

The foam of breaking waves—like piled snow;
blooming peach and plum, silent clusters of spring.

A jar of wine,
silk fishing line.

Is anyone else on earth as happy?

13. 漁父 (2)

一棹春風一葉舟，
一綸繭縷一輕鉤。
花滿渚，
酒滿甌，
萬頃波中得自由。

13. Another to the tune
Fisherman's Song (2)

One oar, spring breeze, boat like a leaf;
fishing line a silken strand, a light hook.

Blossoms cover the islet,
wine brims in the bowl.

Among vast waves, I'm comfortable and free.

14. 蝶戀花
(一題李冠作)

遙夜亭皋閒信步，
乍過清明，
早覺傷春暮。
數點雨聲風約住，
朦朧淡月雲來去。

桃李依依春暗度，
誰在秋千，
笑裏低低語？
一片芳心千萬緒，
人間沒箇安排處。

14. To the tune
Butterflies Lingering Over Flowers

A long night, strolling aimlessly on the shore,
Qingming almost over.
I sense the sadness of spring's end.
A patter of raindrops, checked by the wind,
hazy moonlight, clouds coming and going.

Peach and plum trees cannot bear to part with spring,
    but it sneaks away.
Who's that playing on the rope swing?
Laughing sensually, bowing her head to whisper?
A young woman's feelings are countless, elusive,
no way in this world to settle them.

15. 更漏子
(一題溫庭筠作)

柳絲長，
春雨細，
花外漏聲迢遞。
驚塞雁，
起城烏，
畫屏金鷓鴣。

香霧薄，
透重幕，
惆悵謝家池閣。
紅燭背，
繡幃垂，
夢長君不知。

15. To the tune
Night Song of the Water Clock

Long wands from willows,
thin spring rain;
funneled through flower bushes, the sound spreading far.

Startled geese on the frontier,
crows whirling up from the city wall;
I stare at golden partridges painted on a screen.

Incense mists are thinning,
passing through layers of curtain.
Even those who own mansions and gardens
　　can't escape sadness.

Behind her the flaming red candles,
embroidered curtains hanging down,
as she dreams all night of her lord, who doesn't know.

16. 柳枝

風情漸老見春羞，
到處芳魂感舊遊；
多謝長條似相識，
強垂煙穗拂人頭。

16. To the tune
Willow Branches

Womanly beauty dissipates,
abashed by the sight of spring;
everywhere in the palace I can sense
the soul and shadow of lost memories.

I'm deeply grateful to the willow,
for bringing me the past;
the hanging branches,
dense, brush my head and clear it.

17. 清平樂

別來春半，
觸目愁腸斷。
砌下落梅如雪亂，
拂了一身還滿。

雁來音信無憑，
路遙歸夢難成。
離恨恰如春草，
更行更遠還生。

17. To the tune
Pure Serene Music

Since we said goodbye, spring is half over.
Everywhere I look, I sense a brimming sadness.
Plum blossoms cover the stone steps, like messy snow:
brush them off, they'll just keep coming.

Wild geese overhead, but they bring no news, no letter.
The road is long; the dream of going home—hard to ever
    make happen.
The sorrow of separation is like wild spring grass;
the further we go, the more it flourishes.

18. 阮郎歸 •
呈鄭王十二弟

東風吹水日銜山，
春來長是閑。
落花狼籍酒闌珊，
笙歌醉夢間。

佩聲悄，
晚妝殘，
憑誰整翠鬟？
留連光景惜朱顏，
黃昏獨倚欄。

18. To the tune

Return of a Lover

East winds blow across the water
and the sun sinks to meet the mountains.
Spring is here, we're idle and at leisure.
Fallen blossoms are scattered everywhere,
    empty wine-cups too.
Music and song pervade our drunken dreams.

Sound of a lady's girdle, quiet pendants.
Her evening makeup is a mess.
For whom does she tidy up
in a head-dress with kingfisher feathers?
Take all this in and cherish her beauty
as she leans on the railing, pensive in the twilight.

19. 采桑子

庭前春逐紅英盡，
舞態徘徊。
細雨霏微，
不放雙眉時暫開。

綠窗冷靜芳音斷，
香印成灰。
可奈情懷，
欲睡朦朧入夢來。

19. To the tune
Mulberry-Picking Song

Spring in the courtyard, the blossoms scattered,
drifting about like dancers.
Thin rain, drizzling mist.
Eyes clamped shut, I can see nothing.

I sit alone by the green window, any good news cut off.
Incense is slowly turning to ashes.
My feelings have no outlet.
I fall asleep in hazy moonlight, just as you enter my dreams.

20. 搗練子令

深院靜，
小庭空。
斷續寒砧斷續風。
無奈夜長人不寐，
數聲和月到簾櫳。

20. To the tune
Pounding White Silk

The courtyard depths—so quiet;
and my little garden, deserted.

Sound of the laundry pounding, off and on,
    the wind as well.

The night goes on forever, and I can't fall asleep.

Its sounds join the moonlight at my window.

21. 搗練子令 (2)

雲鬢亂，
晚妝殘。
帶恨眉兒遠岫攢。
斜托香腮春筍嫩，
為誰和淚倚欄干？

21. Another to the tune
Pounding White Silk (2)

Hair unkempt.
Evening makeup fading.

Eyebrows of sorrow, arched like far-off mountains.

Sweet-smelling cheeks, propped on soft palms.

Whom do you weep for, leaning on the balustrade?

22. 三臺令

不寐倦長更，
披衣出戶行。
月寒秋竹冷，
風切夜窗聲。

22. To the tune
Three High Officials

Unable to sleep, tired of the long night,
I get up, put on my coat, go out for a walk.

The moon is wintry above autumn bamboo.
All night a chilly wind rattles the window.

23. 采桑子

轆轤金井梧桐晚，
幾樹驚秋。
晝雨新愁。
百尺蝦鬚在玉鉤。

瓊窗夢斷雙蛾皺，
回首邊頭，
欲寄鱗遊，
九曲寒波不溯流。

23. To the tune
Mulberry-Picking Song

A decorated well with a windlass
    and phoenix trees—late autumn.
How many trees are startled by fall?
Rain all day, enlarging my melancholy.
The shrimp-whisker curtains hang high on jade hooks.

Behind the elegant windows, broken dreams,
    frowning brows.
I twist my head to gaze at distant lands,
wishing I could send letters with the fish,
but the Yellow River's icy currents are too strong for them.

24. 長相思
(一題鄧肅作)

一重山,
兩重山,
山遠天高煙水寒,
相思楓葉丹。

菊花開,
菊花殘,
塞雁高飛人未還,
一簾風月閒。

24. To the tune
Eternal Longing

One range of mountains.
A second range of mountains.
Mountains so distant, sky so high,
    misty waters so cold.
Our love and longing turn the maples scarlet.

Chrysanthemums have bloomed.
Chrysanthemums have withered.
High overhead, the northern geese fly back,
    but you do not return.
I am a hanging blind, stirred by the wind and moon.

25. 謝新恩

秦樓不見吹簫女，
空余上苑風光。
粉英金蕊自低昂。
東風惱我，
才發一襟香。

瓊窗□夢留殘日，
當年得恨何長！
碧欄干外映垂楊。
暫時相見，
如夢懶思量。

25. To the tune
Thankful for New Favors

Gone is the Phoenix Pavilion and the girl who played the
    flute there.
The imperial gardens stand empty and silent.
Blossoms, some pink, float everywhere.
The east wind irritates me,
even though right by the hall
fragrance suddenly fills the air.

As day ends, behind elegant windows I'm more dreaming
    than awake,
revisiting all my old sorrows—how vast can remorse be!
Outside, the jade balconies echo the weeping willows.
Our love could not last long—
like a dream one can't bear to remember.

26. 謝新恩 (2)

櫻花落盡階前月，
象床愁倚薰籠
遠似去年今日，
恨還同。

雙鬟不整雲憔悴，
淚沾紅抹胸。
何處相思苦？
紗窗醉夢中。

26. Another to the tune
Thankful for New Favors (2)

Cherry blossoms scattered by the stairs in moonlight.
She lies on an ivory bed, leaning toward the brazier.
What seems a long time was just a year ago today.
The deep regret's the same.

Her braided hair unravels, an anxious storm cloud.
Tears stain her crimson bodice.
Where else can you find bitterness like this?
Behind her gauze window, drunk on her dreams.

27. 謝新恩 (3)

庭空客散人歸後，
畫堂半掩珠簾。
林風淅淅夜厭厭。
小樓新月，
回首自纖纖。

春光鎮在人空老，
新愁往恨何窮？
金窗力困起還慵。
一聲羌笛，
驚起醉怡容。

27. Another to the tune
Thankful for New Favors (3)

The courtyard's deserted. The guests have disappeared.
The hall of paintings is half closed-off by pearl curtains.
I listen to forest winds all through a tranquil night;
a small pavilion and the new moon—
raising my face to witness its slenderness.

Spring's brightness persists, but people age.
Gloomy feelings and old regrets—where is their end?
Behind the golden window, too tired and lazy to leave.
Sudden notes from a wild Qiang flute—
they startle me from contented drunkenness.

28. 謝新恩 (4)

櫻桃落盡春將困,
秋千架下歸時。
漏暗斜月遲遲,
在花枝。

[Missing 12 characters]

徹曉紗窗下,
待來君不知。

28. Another to the tune
Thankful for New Favors (4)

Cherry season's over, spring is nearly gone;
it's time to come in from the swing.
Everything's quiet, under a tilting moon;
all flowers open on their boughs

[two lines missing]

All night, by the screened window,
waiting for you, but my lord doesn't know.

29. 謝新恩 (5)

冉冉秋光留不住，
滿階紅葉暮。
又是過重陽，
臺榭登臨處，
茱萸香墜。

紫菊氣，
飄庭戶，
晚煙籠細雨。
離離新雁咽寒聲，
愁恨年年長相似。

29. Another to the tune
Thankful for New Favors (5)

The autumn scenery goes—no way to hold it back.
Red leaves pile up on the steps by dusk,
time once more for the Double Ninth Festival.
We can climb to the music hall at the water's edge.
People will be wearing fragrant dogwood blooms.

There's also the odor of purple chrysanthemums
floating through the courtyards and households.
Evening smoke obscures the drizzling rain.
A flock of new geese call tunefully in cold air.
Year after year they persist—my sorrow and regret.

30. 臨江仙

櫻桃落盡春歸去，
蝶翻輕粉雙飛。
子規啼月小樓西，
玉鉤羅幕，
惆悵暮烟垂。

別巷寂寥人散後，
望殘烟草低迷。
爐香閑裊鳳凰兒。
空持羅帶，
回首恨依依。

30. To the tune

Immortal at the River

The cherries are gone—spring's over.
White butterflies float past, up and down, in pairs.
A cuckoo calls to the moon by the west pavilion.
My gauze bed curtains hang from jade hooks.
Evening arrives like smoke and I grow sad.

The narrow lanes are empty
    now that the guests are gone.
I gaze at traces of grass in the mist,
    the sky thick with clouds.
Fragrance curls up slowly
    from the phoenix incense burner.
Idly holding the silk sash of my robe,
I stare into the past, heart filled with regret.

31. 破陣子

四十年來家國，
三千里地山河。
鳳閣龍樓連霄漢，
玉樹瓊枝作烟蘿。
幾曾識干戈？

一旦歸為臣虜，
沈腰潘鬢銷磨。
最是倉皇辭廟日，
教坊猶奏離別歌。
垂淚對宮娥！

31. To the tune
Break Through Enemy Ranks

My country lasted for forty years
in a landscape of mountains and rivers spanning three
    thousand *li*.
With phoenix and dragon patterned palaces,
    sumptuous, that almost touched the sky.
Jade trees and jeweled branches were our foliage.
What did I know about weapons and war?

Once I became a prisoner
my waistline shrank, my hair grew gray.
At the very moment I was saying farewell,
    in panic,
at the royal ancestral shrine,
the court musicians went on playing
    a song of parting and best wishes,
and I wept face to face with the palace maids.

32. 虞美人

風回小院庭蕪綠，
柳眼春相續。
憑欄半日獨無言，
依舊竹聲新月似當年。

笙歌未散尊罍在，
池面冰初解。
燭明香暗畫樓深，
滿鬢清霜殘雪思難任。

32. To the tune
The Beautiful Lady Yu

A spring breeze has come back
    to this overgrown courtyard
and the willow leaves open
    as they always have.
I lean on the balustrade half the day,
    solitary, silent.
As before, sound of bamboo flutes;
    as in bygone days, the new moon.

The playing and singing go on,
    the wine brims in the vessels.
The ice on the pond has begun to crack open.
Bright candles and dim incense
    fill the palace recesses.
At my temples, the hair like frost and snow,
    thoughts too hard to bear.

33. 虞美人 (2)

春花秋月何時了，
往事知多少。
小樓昨夜又東風，
故國不堪回首月明中。

雕欄玉砌應猶在，
只是朱顏改。
問君能有幾多愁，
恰似一江春水向東流。

33. Another to the tune
The Beautiful Lady Yu (2)

Spring flowers, autumn moon: will it ever end?
How much of the past do I still remember?
Last night the east wind blew
    through my small pavilion.
I couldn't bear to look
    back toward my old country
        in the bright moonlight.

All the carved railings and inlaid marble stairs
    are probably still there;
it's just my life, once elegant,
    that's changed so drastically.
You ask how much regret I feel?
Think of a great river, spring-swollen,
    flowing east forever.

34. 望江南

閑夢遠，
南國正芳春。
船上管弦江面綠，
滿城飛絮輥輕塵，
忙殺看花人！

34. To the tune
Gazing South

Idle, dreaming about my distant life.
In my homeland now, it's full and fragrant spring.
Boats with orchestras out on the fresh green river.
The city is filled with floating willow catkins,
    rolling dust,
keeping the flower watchers wildly busy.

35. 望江南 (2)

閑夢遠，
南國正清秋。
千里江山寒色遠，
蘆花深處泊孤舟。
笛在月明樓。

35. Another to the tune
Gazing South (2)

Idle, dreaming about my distant life.
My home county is in full autumn now.
Across a thousand miles of open country,
    cold colors spread far.
Deep in the reeds a solitary boat is moored.
A sad flute plays in a moonlit pavilion.

36. 望江南 (3)

多少恨，
昨夜夢魂中。
還似舊時遊上苑，
車如流水馬如龍；
花月正春風！

36. Another to the tune
Gazing South (3)

So much regret
haunted my dreams last night.
It was like old times again,
    roaming the palace grounds.
Chariots like fast water,
    horses like dragons.
Flowers and moon just right,
    matching the spring breezes.

37. 望江南 (4)

多少淚，
斷臉復橫頤。
心事莫將和淚說，
鳳笙休向淚時吹；
腸斷更無疑！

37. Another to the tune
Gazing South (4)

So many tears—
I dry my cheeks, my chin's still wet.
Crying gets in the way while I'm trying to tell
    of the heavy load in my heart.
And I shouldn't listen to the reed pipe
    when my eyes are full of tears.
I'll only break my heart some more.

38. 相見歡

林花謝了春紅,
太匆匆,
無奈朝來寒雨晚來風;

胭脂淚,
相留醉,
幾時重,
自是人生長恨水長東。

38. To the tune
Joy of Meeting

Spring flowers faded and fallen in the woods;
it's just too rushed,
and as if fated: cold bitter rain all morning,
    wind blowing all night.

Tears mixing with rouge and mascara,
yet we linger—drunken.
When will we meet again?
Life is always full of regret,
    same way the river flows east.

39. 相見歡 (2)

無言獨上西樓，
月如鉤，
寂寞梧桐深院鎖清秋。

剪不斷，
理還亂，
是離愁，
別是一番滋味在心頭。

39. Another to the tune
Joy of Meeting (2)

Silent and alone, I climb to the west pavilion.
The moon is a hook.
The lone wutong tree in the secluded courtyard
    is deep in the autumn chill.

I try to prune my sorrow, but can't cut through it.
I try to order it, but still it tangles.
It's the grief at losing my homeland—
no other feeling in my heart but this.

40. 烏夜啼

昨夜風兼雨，
簾幃颯颯秋聲。
燭殘漏斷頻倚枕。
起坐不能平。

世事漫隨流水，
算來一夢浮生。
醉鄉路穩宜頻到，
此外不堪行。

40. To the tune
Crows Calling at Night

Last night's wind on top of all that rain,
the blowing curtains like the sighing sound of autumn.
The candles burn down, the water clocks stop,
    and still I lie on my pillow.
I got up, I sat down, and still could find no peace.

Life flows on like cascading water—
all of this a dream in a floating world.
When I drink enough, the road is smooth and easy;
otherwise, I can't bear to go down it.

41. 子夜歌 (2)

人生愁恨何能免？
銷魂獨我情何限！
故國夢重歸，
覺來雙淚垂。

高樓誰與上？
長記秋晴望。
往事已成空，
還如一夢中。

41. To the tune
Midnight Songs

No life is free of sorrow and heartache,
but I've had more than my share,
    grief without limits.
In my dream I was back in my homeland
and woke up with my eyes full of tears.

Who will come with me to climb the high tower?
I'll always remember the clear autumn skies
    and gazing off into the distance.
Those days are hollow and empty now,
yet still they return as in a dream.

42. 浪淘沙

往事只堪哀,
對景難排。
秋風庭院蘚侵階。
一任珠簾閒不捲,
終日誰來?

金瑣已沉埋,
壯氣蒿萊。
晚涼天淨月華開。
想得玉樓瑤殿影,
空照秦淮。

42. To the tune
Ripples Sifting Sand

The past offers sadness—
whatever the scene, I can't push it away.

An autumn wind blows through the garden;
    moss overtakes the steps.

The pearl screen hangs loose; no one to roll it up.
All day long nobody will come.

The blockade locks are sunk and buried.
My youthful spirit lies flattened among weeds.

Cool night, clear sky, moon in full bloom.
I remember the jade pavilions,

the precious palaces—
empty reflections in the Qinhuai River.

43. 浣溪沙 (2)

轉燭飄蓬一夢歸，
欲尋陳迹悵人非，
天教心願與身違。

待月池臺空逝水，
蔭花樓閣謾斜暉，
登臨不惜更沾衣。

43. Another to the tune
Sands of the Silk-Washing Stream (2)

Life in this world is a candle in the wind,
drifting duckweed, ending in a dream.

I try to revisit familiar places and people,
but nothing is the same.

The will of heaven never seems
to match my wishes.

I stand by the pond in moonlight;
I watch the indifferent flow of water.

Tall pavilions shade flowering shrubs.
Slanting sunlight fills the air.

I climbed up here to gaze far off,
not caring if tears soaked my clothes.

44. 浪淘沙令

簾外雨潺潺,
春意闌珊。
羅衾不耐五更寒。
夢裏不知身是客,
一餉貪歡。

獨自莫憑欄,
無限江山,
別時容易見時難。
流水落花春去也,
天上人間。

44. To the tune
Ripples Sifting Sand

Beyond the curtains, sound of pattering rain.
Spring is fading fast.
My silken quilt can't stop this pre-dawn cold.
In my dream I didn't know I was just a guest.
I simply enjoyed the moment of happiness.

Alone, I try not to lean on the railing,
    gazing back at my past.
The endless rivers and high mountains.
Easy to say goodbye. Hard to reunite.
The river flows on, the blossoms fall;
    spring passes away.
That's how our world differs from heaven.

NOTES

Our work on Li Yu, 937-978 (李煜; ceremonial name, Li Houzhu 李後主) is based on the online edition of *Nantang erzhu ci* (南唐二主詞).

We consistently use traditional Chinese characters (傳統漢字) and the Chinese Hanyu Pinyin system (漢語拼音).

1. To the tune *Sands of the Silk-Washing Stream*

   • Title in Chinese: Huan xi sha: Hong ri yi gao san zhang tou
   • 6 sentences, 42 characters

   1. Huan xi sha 浣溪沙, a "tune name" of the *ci*.
   2. San zhang 三丈, three of zhang, a unit of length, equivalent to 3.33 meters.
   3. Jin lu 金爐, golden metallic (typically copper) incense burner.
   4. Xiang shou 香獸, charcoal grains (carbon dusts) mixed with spices to form in the shape of animals.
   5. Di yi 地衣, woven fabrics lying on floor (carpet).
   6. Jia ren 佳人, beautiful woman.
   7. Wu dian 舞點, dancing to the tune of music (meter).
   8. Jin chai 金釵, golden hairpin.
   9. Jiu e 酒惡, being intoxicated.
   10. Hua rui 花蕊, stamen and pistil, meaning flowers.
   11. Bie dian 別殿, imperial villa, detached royal court or imperial palace.
   12. Xiao gu 簫鼓, vertical bamboo flute and drum.

2. To the tune *Spring in the Jade Pavilion*

- Title in Chinese: Yulou chun: Wan zhuang chu liao ming ji xue
- 8 sentences, 56 characters

1. Yu lou chun 玉樓春, the tune name of this poem, is also called Mu lan hua 木蘭花 (Magnolia Blossoms).
2. Chun dian 春殿, or yu dian 御殿, a magnificent palace, a royal court.
3. Pin e 嬪娥, women attendants at court.
4. Yu guan 魚貫, one after another, in single file.
5. Sheng xiao 笙簫, reed pipe wind instrument and vertical bamboo flute.
6. Shui yun 水雲, between clouds and waters (rivers, lake, and seas), meaning extreme distance.
7. Ni chang or Ni shang 霓裳, clothing of the immortals, referring to "Ni chang yu yi qu 霓裳羽衣曲 (The Raiment of Rainbows and Feathers Dance)," a masterpiece of song and dance allegedly created by Emperor Xuanzong of Tang (Tang Xuanzong 唐玄宗, 685-762).
8. Bian 遍, segments of da bian 大遍 or da qu 大曲, music originating in Central Asia.
9. Lin chun 臨春, literally, on the point of spring. There was a pavilion named Linchun Ge, 臨春閣, in the royal court of Southern Tang.
10. Xiang xie 香屑, fragrant powder.
11. Lan gan 闌干, banisters, railings.
12. Ma ti 馬蹄, horse's hoof.
13. Qing ye 清夜, in the stillness of night.

3. To the tune *Night Song of the Water Clock*

- Title in Chinese: Genglou zi: Jin que chai hong fen mian
- 12 sentences, 46 characters
- Authorship also attributed to Wen Tingyun 溫庭筠, 812-870, of Tang dynasty (618-907).

1. Jin que chai 金雀釵, decorative hairpin in the shape of a golden sparrow.
2. Hong fen 紅粉, red facial powder, referring to attractive woman.
3. Xiang sui 香穗, smoke of burning incense forming into the ear of wheat image.
4. La lei 蠟淚, oil of burning candle looking like tear drops.
5. Shan zhen 珊枕, shan hu zhen 珊瑚枕, a pillow filled with colorful crushed corals.
6. Jin qin 錦衾, a quilt of silk brocade.
7. Geng lou 更漏, geng 更, a unit of time in ancient China, equivalent to 2 hours; lou 漏 or louhu 漏壺, a type of water clock or clepsydra.

4. To the tune *Deva-like Barbarian*

- Title in Chinese: Pusa man: Hua ming yue an long qing wu
- 8 sentences, 44 characters

1. Long 籠, long zhao 籠罩, to shroud.
2. Lang 郎, lang jun 郎君, husband, lover.
3. Chan 剗, or chan 剷, to level off, to pare down.
4. Jin lü 金縷, gold thread.
5. Hua tang 畫堂, richly ornamented magnificent palace in

royal court.

6. Yi xiang 一向, or yi shang 一晌, a short while.
7. Wei 偎, Wei yi 偎依, to cuddle together, to hug, lean close to.
8. Nu 奴, or nu jia 奴家, meaning bondservant; a woman in ancient China called herself "nu" to express humility.
9. Zi yi 恣意, to do as one pleases, unscrupulous, willful.
10. This was one of the love poems Li Yu wrote (around 964) when he had an affair with the younger sister (Xiao Zhou Hou 小周后, 950-978) of the Empress (Da Zhou Hou 大周后, 936-964).

5. Another to the tune *Bodhisattva-like Barbarian* (2)

- Title in Chinese: Pusa man (2): Peng lai yuan bi tian tai nü
- 8 sentences, 44 characters

1. Peng lai yuan, 蓬萊院, a courtyard as graceful and exquisite as the legendary Penglai island of the immortals (believed to be somewhere off the east coast of China).
2. Tian tai nü, 天台女, legendary fairy maiden of Tiantai Mountain (in present-day Zhejiang province).
3. Cui yun, 翠雲, bluish-green clouds, figuratively meaning a woman's dark, thick hair, like floating clouds.
4. Zhu suo, 珠鎖, door knocker with string of pearls.
5. Yin ping meng, 銀屏夢, a pleasant dream as if looking upon a shimmering panel of a silver-white folding screen.
6. Lian man, 臉慢, or 臉曼, delicate and tender face, beautiful appearance.

6. Another to the tune *Bodhisattva-like Barbarian* (3)

    •   Title in Chinese: Pusa man (3): Tong huang yun cui qiang han zhu
    •   8 sentences, 44 characters

    1. Tong huang, 銅簧, bronze reed instrument.
    2. Zhu, 竹, bamboo, referring to a woodwind instrument.
    3. Xian yu, 纖玉, fine silk embroidery smooth as jade, suggesting a female musician's slender fingers.
    4. Yan se, 眼色, meaningful glance expressing feelings.
    5. Qiu bo, 秋波, autumn ripples, suggesting a beautiful woman's bewitching eyes, clear and bright.
    6. Yu, 欲 or 慾, desires, passion, lust.
    7. Yu yun, 雨雲, or yun yu 雲雨, rain and clouds, figuratively meaning erotic passion.
    8. Xiu hu, 繡戶, an ornamented, elegant residence.
    9. Zhong su, 衷素 or 衷愫, to cherish inner feelings.
    10. Chun meng, 春夢, spring dreams, figuratively meaning transient joys, visionary fancies.

7. To the tune *Joyful Oriole Flies Away*

    •   Title in Chinese: Xi qian ying: Xiao yue zhui
    •   10 sentences, 47 characters

    1. Xiao yue 曉月, moon at daybreak, bright moonlight.
    2. Su yun 宿雲, morning clouds (literally, clouds from the previous night that remain in the morning sky).
    3. Qi 欹, or qi xie 欹斜, crooked, askew, aslant, tilt.
    4. Fang cao 芳草, sweet-smelling grass.

5. Yi yi 依依, unwilling to part, attached.
6. Yan 雁, wild geese. In Chinese legend, wild geese carry letters from a faraway land.
7. Ti ying 啼鶯, calling orioles.
8. Yu hua 餘花, withered flowers.
9. Shen yuan 深院, secluded courtyard.
10. Pian hong 片紅, red pieces, figuratively meaning petals from fallen flowers.

8. To the tune *Eternal Longing*

   - Title in Chinese: Chang xiang si: Yun yi wo
   - 8 sentences, 36 characters
   - One of Li Yu's best-known poems.

1. Yun 雲, Yun ji 雲髻 or ji yun 髻雲, a cloud-like coiffeur, in which the strands of hair are coiled into a chignon.
2. Wo 緺, 渦, or 窩, nest; also pronounced gua 緺, meaning cord, silk ribbon, or braid.
3. Yu 玉, yu zen or yu zan 玉簪, jade hairpin.
4. Suo 梭, a weaver's shuttle.
5. Shan 衫, upper garment.
6. Luo 羅, luo qun 羅裙, thin silk skirt.
7. Pin 顰, to frown.
8. Dai luo 黛螺, bluish-green color, referring to a woman's eyebrows.
9. Ba jiao 芭蕉, banana (likely the species *Musca lasiocarpa*).
10. Nai he 奈何, "What alternative is there?"

9. To the tune *A Casket of Pearls*

- Title in Chinese: Yi hu zhu: Wan zhuang chu guo
- 10 sentences, 57 characters

1. Chen tan 沈檀, or 沉檀, referring to chen xiang mu 沉香木 (agarwood) and tan mu 檀木 (sandalwood), used to make fragrant lipsticks.
2. Qing zhu 輕注, to draw lightly.
3. Xie er ge 些兒箇, a very little.
4. Ding xiang 丁香, lilac, referring to a woman's tongue.
5. Ke 顆, tooth.
6. Qing ge 清歌, song sung as a solo.
7. Ying tao 櫻桃, cherries, referring to a woman's lips and mouth.
8. Po 破, open up or break open.
9. Luo xiu 羅袖, thin silk sleeves.
10. Yi 裛, fragrant.
11. Yin se 殷色, dark red.
12. Ke 可, blurred, indistinct.
13. Xiang lao 香醪, good quality wine.
14. Wan 浣, to wash away.
15. Xiu chuang 繡床, a bed covered with embroideries.
16. Wu nuo 無那, or wu nai 無奈, meaning there is no recourse.
17. Lan jiao 爛嚼, finely chewed to shreds.
18. Hong rong 紅茸, reddish wildflowers that are soft, almost fluffy.
19. Tan lang 檀郎, a sobriquet of the poet Pan Yue 潘岳 (247-300) of Jin dynasty (266-420), who was known for his dashing looks. It is used to refer to a woman's lover or husband.

10. To the tune *Midnight Songs*

- Title in Chinese: Ziye ge: Xun chun xu shi xian chun zao
- 8 sentences, 44 characters

1. Zi ye ge 子夜歌, *Midnight Songs*, referring to a collection of poems by various poets and associated with the folk tradition, compiled during the Jin 晉 dynasty (266-420); see also note to Poem 41.
2. Piao se 縹色, light blue, referring to the color of wine.
3. Yu rou 玉柔, jade-like but soft and tender, referring to a woman's hands.
4. Pei 醅, unstrained spirits, referring to wine in general.
5. Zhan 盞, a small cup.
6. He fang 何妨, meaning "Why not? Why does it matter?"
7. Can 粲, to laugh boisterously.
8. Jin yuan 禁苑, royal garden.
9. Jie gu 羯鼓, a small Chinese double-headed drum struck with two sticks, originally from the Central Asian region of Kucha (present-day Kuqa 庫車) and popular during the Tang dynasty (618-907).

11. To the tune *Flowers of the Inner Court*

- Title in Chinese: Hou ting hua po zi: Yu shu hou ting qian
- 7 sentences, 32 characters
- Authorship also attributed to Feng Yansi 馮延巳 (903-960), or 馮延嗣, also Feng Yanji 馮延己, of Southern Tang dynasty (937-976).

1. Yu shu 玉樹, a tree of jade, associated with fantastical realms

of the immortals.

2. Hou ting 後庭, or hou gong 後宮, the women's part of the inner court of the palace.

3. Yao cao 瑤草, lush grass or fragrant herbs—the likes of which might be found in immortal realms.

4. Pian 偏, inclined to one side, partial, prejudiced.

5. He 和, to harmonize.

6. Jiao 教, to cause, to allow.

12. To the tune *Fisherman's Song*

- Title in Chinese: Yufu: Lang hua you yi qian chong xue
- 5 sentences, 27 characters

1. Lang hua 浪花, the foam of breaking waves.

2. Qian chong 千重, piling up, tier upon tier.

3. Tao li 桃李, flowers or trees of peach and plum.

4. Yi dui 一隊, a file of soldiers.

5. Lun 綸, silken threads, here meaning a fishing line.

6. Nong 儂, during ancient times in China it was used as the first personal pronoun ("I, me"); also meaning "you" in the Wu Chinese dialect (Shanghai, Southern Jiangsu, and Zhejiang Region).

13. Another to the tune *Fisherman's Song* (2)

- Title in Chinese: Yufu (2): Yi zhao chun feng yi ye zhou
- 5 sentences, 27 characters

1. These two "Yu fu" poems (12 and 13) were written as an

inscription on a painting by Wei Xian (衛賢, active 10th century) entitled "Chunjiang diaosou tu" 春江釣叟圖.

2. Zhao 棹, 櫂, an oar.
3. Ye 葉, a leaf or light as a leaf.
4. Jian lü 繭縷, the cocoon of the silkworm, a strand of hair.
5. Gou 鉤, a hook.
6. Zhu 渚, an islet.
7. Ou 甌, a deep bowl.
8. Wan qing 萬頃, ten thousand of "qing," a unit of area measurement, about 15.13 acres.

14. To the tune *Butterflies Lingering Over Flowers*

- Title in Chinese: Dielian hua: Yao ye ting gao
- 10 sentences, 60 characters
- Authorship also attributed to Li Guan (李冠, fl. 1019).

1. Yao ye 遙夜, a long night.
2. Ting gao 亭皋 or 庭皋, flat land edged by water.
3. Xin bu 信步, aimless wandering, sauntering.
4. Zha 乍, suddenly, abruptly.
5. Qing ming 清明, Clear and Bright Festival, traditional tomb-sweeping day, about April 5th.
6. Mu 暮, the end of a period of time.
7. Yue 約, to bind, to restrain.
8. Meng long 朦朧, obscure, ambiguous, to deceive.
9. Yi yi 依依, to be near to, to depend on, unwilling to part from.
10. An du 暗渡, secretly crossing.
11. Qiu qian 秋千, literally autumn/thousand; a homonym for 鞦韆, a rope swing.

12. Fang xin 芳心, feelings of a young woman.
13. Xu 緒, a clue, thoughts, intentions.
14. An pai 安排, to arrange.

15. To the tune *Night Song of the Water Clock*

- Title in Chinese: Genglou zi (2): Liu si chang
- 12 sentences, 46 characters
- Authorship also attributed to Wen Tingyun 溫庭筠, 812-870, of Tang dynasty (618-907).

1. Liu si 柳絲, willow tree wands.
2. Lou sheng 漏聲, sound of a funnel.
3. Tiao di 迢遞, far off.
4. Sai yan 塞雁, geese along the distant frontier, referring to those who are far away from their home regions.
5. Cheng wu 城烏, or cheng tou wu ya 城頭烏鴉, crows perched on the top of city walls or ramparts.
6. Hua ping 畫屏, painting done on a standing screen.
7. Zhe gu 鷓鴣, a partridge.
8. Xiang wu 香霧, fragrant mists.
9. Bo 薄, thin, diminished.
10. Mu 幕, or mo 幙, a curtain.
11. Chou chang 惆悵, disappointed, disconsolate, melancholy.
12. Xie jia chi ge 謝家池閣, refers to the prominent clan of Xie Tiao 謝朓, 464-49; chige (literally, ponds and pavilions) means a wealthy family's mansion and its gardens.
13. Xiu wei 繡幃 or xiu lian 繡簾, embroidered curtains, meaning women's apartments.
14. Meng chang 夢長, a lengthy dream, or meng jun 夢君, dreaming of my lord.

16. To the tune *Willow Branches*

- Title in Chinese: Liuzhi: Feng qing jian lao jian chun xiu
- 4 sentences, 28 characters

1. This poem is also under the title: Si gong ren Qing-nu 賜宮人慶奴, Bestowed on Qing-nu, the Imperial Concubine.
2. Feng qing 風情, elegant demeanor, referring to the appearance of a woman and implying seductive attractiveness for a lover.
3. Fang hun 芳魂, a beautiful woman's soul.
4. Gan 感, gan huai 感懷, to recall with emotion.
5. Jiu you 舊遊, to revisit a once familiar place.
6. Chang tiao 長條, long branch of a willow tree.
7. Yan sui 煙穗, a weeping willow's dense branches.

17. To the tune *Pure Serene Music*

- Title in Chinese: Qingping yue: Bie lai chun ban
- 8 sentences, 46 characters

1. Li Yu wrote this poem in remembering his younger brother Li Congshan 李從善, 940-987, who was sent as a hostage to the powerful Song dynasty in 971.
2. Chu mu 觸目, to strike the eyes, meet the eye, can be seen everywhere.
3. Chou chang 愁腸, pent-up feelings of sadness; anxious forebodings that twist and turn in the mind with no relief.
4. Qi 砌, a stone step.
5. Hai 還, still, even more.
6. Yan 雁, wild goose, legendary carrier of letters.

7. Gui meng 歸夢, a dream of returning home.
8. Li hen 離恨, regret from having parted for a long period.

18. To the tune *Return of a Lover*

- Title in Chinese: Ruan lang gui: Dong feng chui shui ri xian shan
- 9 sentences, 47 characters

1. Ruan lang 阮郎, i.e., Ruan Zhao 阮肇, fl. 58-75 AD, of Eastern Han dynasty (25-220 AD). In legend, he became an immortal and a symbol for a lover married to a beautiful woman.
2. Zheng Wang 鄭王, Prince Zheng, real name Li Congshan 李從善 (940-987), Li Yu's 12th younger brother.
3. Chui shui 吹水, or lin shui 臨水, overlooking the edge of the water.
4. Xian 銜, xian jie 銜接, link up, join.
5. Lang ji 狼籍, or 狼藉, scattered about profusely.
6. Lan shan 闌珊, waning, coming to an end, decayed, worn out, spread in confusion.
7. Sheng ge 笙歌, music and singing.
8. Pei 佩, or 珮, girdle ornaments; huan pei 環佩, or 環珮, a lady's girdle with pendants.
9. Qiao 悄, quiet, silent, gently, softly.
10. Can 殘, a remnant, residue, in a mess.
11. Cui huan 翠環, or 翠鬟, a head-dress adorned with kingfisher feathers.
12. Liu lian 留連, to stop at.
13. Guang jing 光景, circumstances, prospect.
14. Zhu yan 朱顏, hong yan 紅顏, beautiful woman, brimming

with youthfulness and with applied makeup.

15. Yi lan 倚欄, to lean against the railing.

19. To the tune *Mulberry-Picking Song*

- Title in Chinese: Caisang zi: Ting qian chun zhu
- 8 sentences, 44 characters

1. Chun zhu 春逐, spring scenery that follows winter.
2. Hong ying 紅英, hong hua 紅花, red flowers.
3. Pai huai 徘徊, pace up and down.
4. Fei wei 霏微, thin, misty drizzle of rain or snow.
5. Fang yin 芳音, jia yin 佳音, good tidings, welcome news.
6. Xiang yin 香印, or yin xiang 印香, fragrant incense.
7. Ke nai 可奈, wu ke nai he 無可奈何, to have no way out or recourse.
8. Qing huai 情懷, feelings.
9. Meng long 朦朧, hazy moonlight, obscure, dim.

20. To the tune *Pounding White Silk*

- Title in Chinese: Dao lianzi ling: Shen yuan jing
- 5 sentences, 27 characters

1. Lian zi 練子, soft white silk.
2. Shen yuan 深院, or shen zhai da yuan 深宅大院, imposing dwellings and spacious courtyards, a compound of connecting dwelling quarters and courtyards.
3. Duan xu 斷續, off and on.
4. Han zhen 寒砧, cold hammering block for softening silk

fibers.

5. Wu nai 無奈, wu ke nai he 無可奈何, have no way out, there is no alternative.
6. Bu mei 不寐, unable to fall asleep.
7. He yue 和月, to accompany the moon.
8. Lian long 簾櫳, windows.

21. Another to the tune *Pounding White Silk* (2)

- Title in Chinese: Dao lianzi ling (2): Yun bin luan
- 5 sentences, 27 characters

1. Yun bin 雲鬢, cloud-like coiffure featuring hair puffed out at the side.
2. Wan zhuang 晚妝, evening makeup.
3. Yuan xiu 遠岫, faraway mountains; xiu, mountain cave or cavernous peak.
4. Cuan 攢, to assemble, to crowd together.
5. Xie tuo 斜托, to support the chin with hands.
6. Xiang sai 香腮, (a young woman's) sweet, fragrant cheek.
7. Chun sun 春筍, bamboo shoots of the spring.
8. He lei, or huo lei 和淚, to mix with tears.

22. To the tune *Three High Officials*

- Title in Chinese: San tai ling: Bu mei juan chang geng
- 4 sentences, 20 characters

1. This poem was written after Li Yu became a captive of the Song dynasty in 975.

2. San tai 三臺, three high positions of officialdom.
3. Bu mei 不寐, unable to fall asleep.
4. Chang geng 長更, long nightly hours.
5. Qiu zhu 秋竹, autumn's bamboo.
6. Feng qie 風切, winds that pierce.

23. To the tune *Mulberry-Picking Song*

- Title in Chinese: Caisang zi (2): Lu lu jin jing wu tong wan
- 8 sentences, 44 characters

1. Li Yu's younger brother Li Congshan (李從善) was held hostage by the emperor of the Song dynasty after being sent north as part of a tribute mission in 963. In this poem, Li Yu expresses longing for his brother. See also Poem 17.
2. Lu lu 轆轤, a windlass, a pulley.
3. Jin jing 金井, an ornately decorated well in the royal garden. The phrase jin jing, along with wu tong (see below), also imply the season of late autumn.
4. Wu tong 梧桐, species of ree, *Sterculia platanifolia*. According to legend, it is said to be the only tree on which the phoenix will rest.
5. Xin chou 新愁, surprised and saddened by the coming of autumn.
6. Bai chi 百尺, hundred chi (unit), implying it's very long.
7. Xia xu 蝦鬚, shrimp's whiskers, meaning window curtains.
8. Qiong chuang 瓊窗, elegantly decorated windows.
9. Shuang e 雙蛾, the eyebrows of a beautiful woman.
10. Bian tou 邊頭, remote and distant place.
11. Lin you 鱗遊, swimming fish, imagined to be carriers of letters.

12. Jiu qu 九曲, the nine curves of the Yellow River.
13. Su liu 溯流, adverse currents or to move against the current.

24. To the tune *Eternal Longing*

- Title in Chinese: Chang xiang si (2): Yi chong shan
- 8 sentences, 36 characters
- Authorship also attributed to Deng Su 鄧肅,1091-1132, a Song dynasty (960-1279) government official.

1. Chong 重, a layer.
2. Yan shui 煙水, misty waters.
3. Xiang si 相思, mutual love, to be in love, thinking of each other with love.
4. Feng ye 楓葉, maple leaves, a symbol of autumn.
5. Sai yan 塞雁, geese beyond the northern borders.
6. Lian 簾, a curtain, or a hanging screen.
7. Feng yue 風月, sound of the wind and shining of the moon.

25. To the tune *Thankful for New Favors*

- Title in Chinese: Xie xinen: Qin lou bu jian chui xiao nü
- 10 sentences, 58 characters

1. The five poems under this title "Xie xin en 謝新恩" were written by Li Yu in remembrance of his first wife, the Empress Da Zhou hou 大周后, Queen Zhou the Elder, ca. 936-964.
2. Qin lou 秦樓, a pavilion built by Qin Mu Gong 秦穆公 (Duke Mu of Qin, 683-621 BC) for his daughter Princess Nongyu 弄玉. Also called Fenglou 鳳樓 Phoenix Pavilion.

3. Chui xiao nü 吹簫女, flute-playing girl, implying a reference to Princess Nongyu.
4. Shang yuan 上苑, imperial garden and forest.
5. Feng guang 風光, scenery.
6. Fen ying jin rui 粉英金蕊, pink fresh flowers as well as other colorful flowers.
7. Jin 襟, the lapel of a garment, also meaning the space in front of a large hall.
8. □ meng □夢: some editions suggest the phrase may be "meng xing 夢醒," a waking dream.
9. Bi lan gan 碧欄干, a green baluster/railing.
10. Chui yang 垂楊, weeping willow.
11. Si liang 思量, remember, meditate, to be in love with.

26. Another to the tune *Thankful for New Favors* (2)

- Title in Chinese: Xie xinen (2): Ying hua luo jin jie qian yue
- 8 sentences, 44 characters

1. Ying hua 櫻花, cherry tree, cherry blossom.
2. Xiang chuang 象床, ivory bed.
3. yi 倚, to lean towards.
4. Xun long 薰籠, a brazier, a frame for placing over a brazier.
5. Shuang huan 雙鬟, a hairstyle that knots the hair in two circles on top of the head.
6. Yun 雲, clouds, cloudy, dark clouds.
7. Qiao cui 憔悴, haggard from grief or anxiety, wan and sallow, thin and pallid, withered.
8. Zhan 沾, damp, wet.
9. Mo xiong 抹胸, a tight garment for women worn over the breasts. Also called dou du 兜肚 or du dou 肚兜, a kind of

corset.

10. Sha chuang 紗窗, a gauze window to keep out insects.
11. Zui meng 醉夢, a drunken sleep.

27. Another to the tune *Thankful for New Favors* (3)

- Title in Chinese: Xie xinen (3): Ting kong ke san ren gui hou
- 10 sentences, 58 characters

1. Hua tang 畫堂, a palace hall decorated with colorful paintings.
2. Zhu lian 珠簾, curtains decorated with pearls.
3. Xi xi 淅淅, sound of the wind.
4. Yan yan 厭厭, lingering, very long, tranquility.
5. Hsien hsien 纖纖, fine, slender, delicately formed.
6. Zhen 鎮, often, always, just.
7. He qiong 何窮, endless.
8. Jin chuang 金窗, luxuriously decorated windows of a palace.
9. Hai 還, further, continuing.
10. Yong 慵, lazy, indolent.
11. Qiang di 羌笛, Qiang-style flute. Qiang, an ethnically non-Chinese domain in what is present-day western China and the region of Tibet.
12. Zui yi rong 醉怡容, a face flushed from drinking wine and with a happy or contented expression.

28. Another to the tune *Thankful for New Favors* (4)

- Title in Chinese: Xie xinen (4): Ying tao luo jin chun jiang kun
- 8 sentences, 44 characters

1. Ying tao 櫻桃, cherry (fruits).
2. Kun 困, predicament, be hard pressed, fatigued.
3. Qiu qian 秋千, a homonym for 鞦韆, a swing (seat); see Poem 14.
4. Lou an 漏暗, time measuring device (a clepsydra) relying on the flow of water, used in ancient China; the phrase suggests the quietness of night.
5. Che xiao 徹曉, from sunset to sunrise, throughout the night.
6. Sha chuang 紗窗, screen window.
7. Dai lai 待來, to wait for, await.

29. Another to the tune *Thankful for New Favors* (5)

- Title in Chinese: Xie xinen (5): Ran ran qiu guang liu bu zhu
- 10 sentences, 51 characters

1. Ran ran 冉冉, slowly, gradually.
2. Qiu guang 秋光, autumn scenery, sights and sounds of autumn.
3. Chong Yang 重陽, Chong Yang Jie 重陽節, Chong Yang Festival or Double Ninth Festival. It occurs on the ninth day of the ninth month of the Lunar calendar. It is also called Senior Citizens' Day.
4. Tai xie 臺榭, halls for the performance of songs and dances, water-side pavilion.
5. Zhu yu 茱萸, dogwood. (Zhu 茱, also pronounced as shu.)
6. Xiang zhui 香墜, fragrant pendant.
7. Zi ju 紫菊, purple chrysanthemum.
8. Yong yong 雝雝, harmonious, tinkling. (Yong 雝, same as 雍.)
9. Chou hen 愁恨, grieving, melancholy, regret.

30. To the tune *Immortal at the River*

- Title in Chinese: Linjiang xian: Ying tao luo jin chun gui qu
- 10 sentences, 58 characters

1. Die fan 蝶翻, butterflies floating up and down.
2. Qing fen 輕粉, soft white butterfly.
3. Zi gui 子規, or du juan 杜鵑, cuckoo, the large hawk-cuckoo.
4. Yu gou 玉鉤, jade hook.
5. Luo mu 羅幕, silk gauze tent or bed-curtain.
6. Chou chang 惆悵, disconsolate, melancholy.
7. Bie xiang 別巷, small lanes of exceptional charm.
8. Ji liao 寂寥, lonesome, desolate, vacant.
9. Wang can 望殘, remnant, a surviving trace.
10. Xian niao 閑裊, leisurely and carefree, slender and delicate.
11. Feng huang er 鳳凰兒, objects with a design incorporating the motif of a phoenix.
12. Luo dai 羅帶, silk gauze belt.
13. Hui shou 回首, to recollect, to look back.
14. Yi yi 依依, lingering emotions, reluctant to part.

31. To the tune *Break Through Enemy Ranks*

- Title in Chinese: Po zhenzi: Si shi nian lai
- 10 sentences, 62 characters
- One of Li Yu's best-known poems.

1. Li 里, a unit of distance in ancient China, about one-half kilometer.
2. Feng ge long lou 鳳閣龍樓, palace buildings and pavilions

with phoenix and dragon motifs, implying a splendid imperial residence.

3. Xiao han 霄漢, the sky, the firmament.
4. Yu shu qiong zhi 玉樹瓊枝, magnificent trees and jeweled branches.
5. Yan luo 烟蘿, dense woods mingled with usnea moss, meaning luxuriant foliage.
6. Gan ge 干戈, weaponry, meaning war and military campaign.
7. Shen yao 沈腰, Shen referring to Shen Yue 沈約 (441-513), a poet and historian who held official positions during the period of three dynasties (Liu Song dynasty, the Southern Qi dynasty, and the Liang dynasty), known as the Southern Dynasties (420-589). Shen was well-known for his thin waistline due to illness.
8. Pan bin 潘鬢, Pan referring to Pan Yue 潘岳 (247-300), a poet who served as an official under the Jin dynasty (266-420). Pan was famous for his good looks, so people noticed when his hair turned gray.
9. Xiao mo, 銷磨 or 消磨, wear down, fritter away.
10. Cang huang 倉皇, in panic.
11. Ci miao 辭廟, bid farewell to the ancestral temple of a ruling house.
12. Jiao fang 教坊, workshop, music studio.
13. Gong e 宮娥, a maid in a royal court.

32. To the tune *The Beautiful Lady Yu*

- Title in Chinese: Yu meiren: Feng hui xiao yuan ting wu lü
- 8 sentences, 56 characters

1. Ting wu 庭蕪, overgrown weeds in the courtyard.

2. Liu yan 柳眼, eyes of the willow, meaning tender leaves.
3. Zhu sheng 竹聲, bamboo wind instruments.
4. Sheng ge 笙歌, playing and singing.
5. Zun lei 尊罍, valuable, urn-shaped wine vessels.
6. Hua lou 畫樓, a gorgeous palace.

33. Another to the tune *The Beautiful Lady Yu* (2)

- Title in Chinese: Yu meiren (2): Chun hua qiu yue he shi liao
- 8 sentences, 56 characters
- One of Li Yu's best-known poems.

1. Wang shi 往事, memories of the past.
2. Gu guo 故國, the motherland, one's home country.
3. Bu kan hui shou 不堪回首, cannot bear to look back.
4. Diao lan yu qi 雕欄玉砌, carved balustrades and marble steps.
5. Zhu yan 朱顏, a woman's graceful looks, figuratively implying a previous life of luxury.
6. Yi jiang 一江, the gigantic river, i.e., the Yangtze River.

34. To the tune *Gazing South*

- Title in Chinese: Wang Jiangnan: Xian meng yuan, nan guo zheng fang chun
- 5 sentences, 27 characters

1. Jiang Nan 江南, or Jiangnan, literally "south of the Yangtze River," encompassing modern-day southern Jiangsu, northern Zhejiang, parts of Anhui, and Jiangxi Provinces.

2. Nan guo 南國, southern kingdom, reffering to Li Yu's home state and the territory of the Southern Tang dynasty.
3. Guan xian 管弦, orchestra or musical ensemble.
4. Fei xu 飛絮, willow catkins flying in the air.
5. Gun 輥, roller, rolling in quick motion.
6. Mang sha 忙殺, exceedingly busy.

35. Another to the tune *Gazing South* (2)

- Title in Chinese: Wang Jiangnan (2): Xian meng yuan, nan guo zheng qing qiu
- 5 sentences, 27 characters

1. Qing qiu 清秋, autumn at its height.
2. Qian li 千里, thousand *li* [unit], suggesting a vast landmass.
3. Jiang shan 江山, rivers and mountains, meaning a landscape or territory of such topographical features.
4. Lu hua 蘆花, reed catkins.
5. Di 笛, flute, the plaintive sound of a flute, indicating the sadness of farewell or separation.

36. Another to the tune *Gazing South* (3)

- Title in Chinese: Wang Jiangnan (3): Duo shao hen
- 5 sentences, 27 characters

1. Meng hun 夢魂, a dreamland, an illusory dream.
2. Shang yuan 上苑, an imperial garden.
3. Hua yue 花月, flowers and moon, indicating pleasant scenery.

37. Another to the tune *Gazing South* (4)

- Title in Chinese: Wang Jiangnan (4): Duo shao lei
- 5 sentences, 27 characters

1. Duan lian 斷臉, to wipe away tears from the face.
2. Heng yi 橫頤, (tears) crossing the chin.
3. Xin shi 心事, heavy burden of worry.
4. Feng sheng 鳳笙, a phoenix-shaped wind instrument.
5. Chang duan 腸斷, heartbroken.

38. To the tune *Joy of Meeting*

- Title in Chinese: Xiangjian huan: Lin hua xie liao chun hong
- 7 sentences, 36 characters

1. Lin hua 林花, flowers in the forest.
2. Xie 謝, or diao xie 凋謝, blossoms faded and fallen.
3. Chun hong 春紅, spring flowers.
4. Cong cong 匆匆, or cong mang 匆忙, hurriedly, precipitately.
5. Wu nai 無奈, nothing to do—no recourse.
6. Yan zhi lei 胭脂淚, women's tears; Yan zhi 胭脂, cosmetics, makeup.
7. Zui 醉, or xin zui 心醉, infatuated with.
8. Chong 重, or chong feng 重逢, to meet again.
9. Zi shi 自是, ought to be, it naturally is.
10. Chang hen 長恨, a long time of regret.

39. Another to the tune *Joy of Meeting* (2)

- Title in Chinese: Xiangjian huan (2): Wu yan du shang xi lou
- 7 sentences, 36 characters

1. Wu yan 無言, speechless, silently.
2. Wu tong 梧桐, Wutong tree, or *Firmiana simplex*, originating in China and Japan.
3. Suo qing qiu 鎖清秋, qing qiu 清秋, or shen qiu 深秋, the height of autumn—immersed in a sense of that.
4. Li 理, zheng li 整理, to put in order, to adjust.
5. Luan 亂, za luan 雜亂, disorderly, mixed up.
6. Li chou 離愁, grief at or sorrow of separation, sorrow of departing from one's home country.

40. To the tune *Crows Calling at Night*

- Title in Chinese: Wu ye ti: Zuo ye feng jian yu
- 8 sentences, 47 characters

1. Jian 兼, concurrently.
2. Lian wei 簾幃, a screen, a curtain, (bamboo) blinds.
3. Sa sa 颯颯, soughing or whistling sound as made by the wind in the trees.
4. Zhu can 燭殘, candles burning to remnants.
5. Lou duan 漏斷, deep into the late hours of night. Lou 漏, lou hu 漏壺, or di lou 滴漏, a kind of shui zhong 水鐘, water clock, old-fashioned time piece, clepsydra. See Poems 3 and 28.
6. Yi 倚, leaning on, resting on.
7. Ping 平, ping jing 平靜, peace and tranquility.

8. Shi shi 世事, worldly affairs, the affairs of life.
9. Man 漫, casual, unrestrained, free.
10. Suan lai 算來, to consider as.
11. Fu sheng 浮生, a floating life.
12. Zui xiang 醉鄉, a state of drunkenness.

41. To the tune *Midnight Songs*

   • Title in Chinese: Ziye ge (2): Ren sheng chou hen he neng
     mian
   • 8 sentences, 44 characters

1. Zi ye ge 子夜歌, Midnight Songs; see Poem 10.
2. Chou hen 愁恨, you chou 憂愁, melancholy, grieving; and
    yuan hen 怨恨, hatred, animosity, resentment.
3. Xiao hun 銷魂, or xiao hun 消魂, haunted by love or
    extreme sadness.
4. He xian 何限, synonymous with wu xian 無限, unlimited.
5. Chang ji 長記, to remember forever.
6. Qiu qing 秋晴, clear skies of autumn.
7. Wang 望, tiao wang 眺望, to gaze at.
8. Wang shi 往事, bygone days, memories of the past.
9. Kong 空, illusory, empty.
10. Hai 還, still, yet.

42. To the tune *Ripples Sifting Sand*

   • Title in Chinese: Langtao sha: Wang shi zhi kan ai
   • 10 sentences, 54 characters

1. Pai 排, pai qian 排遣, dissipate, to push away.
2. Xian 蘚, tai xian 苔蘚, moss, lichen.
3. Ren 任, ren ping 任憑, to let a person/thing take his/its course.
4. Xian 閒, idleness, leisure.
5. Jin suo 金鎖, metal locks used for a blockade.
6. Hao lai 蒿萊, literally a jungle of vegetal growth, implying an emotional state that is defeated, battered down.
7. Yue hua 月華, a lunar corona.
8. Qin huai He 秦淮河, the Qinhuai River, a tributary of the Yangtze which flows through central Nanjing. It was a bustling and flourishing district of the national capital Jinling (金陵, present Nanjing 南京) during Li Yu's rule over the Nan Tang 南唐 dynasty.

43. Another to the tune *Sands of the Silk-Washing Stream* (2)

- Title in Chinese: Huan xi sha (2): Zhuan zhu piao peng yi meng gui
- 6 sentences, 42 characters

1. Zhuan zhu 轉燭, a wind-blown candle, implying unpredictability.
2. Piao peng 飄蓬, drifting duckweeds.
3. Chen ji 陳跡, relics, things of the past.
4. Chang 悵, chang wang 悵惘, disappointed, dejected.
5. Jiao 教, yielding.
6. Dai yue 待月, waiting for moonrise, implying lovers' secret tryst in the midnight hours.
7. Chi tai 池台, chi yuan 池苑 a pond or moat in an estate's garden; lou tai 樓台 a pavilion on the upper level of a

118

structure.

8. Shi shui 逝水, flowing water, figuratively meaning bygone days or events.
9. Yin 蔭, shade, shady, damp and chilly; yin bi 蔭蔽, to be shaded by foliage, to cover, to conceal.
10. Man 謾, or 漫, mi man 瀰漫, to be present all over, to permeate, to penetrate.
11. Xie hui 斜暉, slanting sun rays.
12. Zhan 沾, zhan shi 沾濕 damp, wet garments.

44. To the tune *Ripples Sifting Sand*

- Title in Chinese: Huan xi sha (2): Zhuan zhu piao peng yi meng gui
- 6 sentences, 42 characters
- One of Li Yu's best-known poems.

1. Chan chan 潺潺, babble, murmur, patter.
2. Lan shan 闌珊, waning, coming to an end.
3. Luo qin 羅衾, silk gauze quilt.
4. Wu geng 五更, the fifth and last watch just before dawn.
5. Shang 晌, certain time of day.
6. Ping lan 憑欄, lean on the railing (and gaze into the distance).
7. Jiang shan 江山, the land; often referring to the territory of a state.
8. Liu shui 流水, flowing water.
9. Tian shang 天上, sky, heaven.
10. Ren jian 人間, the world of mortals, the human world.

Milton Keynes UK
Ingram Content Group UK Ltd.
UKHW040857020124
435341UK00001B/38